To the Cross

MICHAEL JUSTIN DAVIS

TO THE
CROSS

A Sequence of Dramatic Poems

WITH WOOD ENGRAVINGS BY
Simon Brett

First published in Great Britain 1991
SPCK
Holy Trinity Church
Marylebone Road
London NW1 4DU

First published in 1984 by Paulinus Press,
12 Blowhorn Street, Marlborough, Wilts SN8 1BT

British Library Cataloguing in Publication Data

Davis, Michael *1925–*
To the cross.
1. English poetry
I. Title
821.914

ISBN 0-281-04545-3

Printed in Great Britain by
The Longdunn Press Ltd, Bristol

To Lis and Miriam Evans

Preface to New Edition

To the Cross was commissioned for presentation in Salisbury Cathedral during Holy Week, 1983, and was given a first performance there on March 28 that year, by Richard Evans, Bernard Finch, David Horlock, Graham Rees and Caroline Swift, actors from the Salisbury Playhouse Company under the direction of David Horlock, with music composed by Michael Lunts.

Since then, there have been many performances in a wide variety of churches and schools. The text seems to make no rigid demands on directors and designers. Greatly differing styles of presentation have proved equally successful.

Individuals or groups contemplating performance of *To the Cross* may feel free to make their own selection from among the eighteen poems in the sequence. Permission for public performances, in whole or in part, should be obtained from SPCK, Holy Trinity Church, Marylebone Road, London NW1 4DU

The Speakers

I carry out orders
And I don't ask questions.
When there's a man to be crucified,
I crucify him.
Yes, of course it's a horrible death.
Yes, some do call it the cruellest of all;
And well, yes: I am a bit of an expert.

But none of these criminals
Is a Roman, is he?
If he was, he'd be too good
For crucifixion.
It's only foreign scum
Who get these nails banged
Through their wrists
And are then hung up there
For hours and hours and hours,
Dying.

A SOLDIER 1

Deserve it? What do you mean?
I'm not interested. I've got a job to do.
Yes, I'm the lad who hammers the nails.
First we lay him on the ground,
See, and we shove
A cross-beam under his shoulders,
And I bash the nails into his wrists.
Sometimes I'm ordered to tie
Him on instead with rope, wrists and ankles.
I pretend it's my choice, make a joke of it
With him: but I much prefer nails, myself.

Anyway,
My mates hoist him up and fix
The cross-beam onto the upright.
That's their job.
Quite low. Our commander likes the face
To be within spitting distance.
Always at the ready, the uprights are,
Stuck in the rock.
We don't waste time at Calvary.

I keep an extra long nail ready
For his feet
And the moment he's hoisted up
I slam it in.
Comes with practice. It's really a knack.
Then between spells on watch – very boring –
Off we go to other routine duties:
Till I get the order to come back
And break his legs.
With my metal club. Specially made.
Oh, they take days, quite often.
Sometimes I never get an order at all:
He just carries on, in his own time.

A real nuisance, when we need

Every cross there is room for on Calvary.
They say the ground is shaped like a skull,
But it sounds a bit fancy to me.
Stoning to death? That's the Jewish way.
Much quicker. But primitive, very crude.
Yes, never a dull moment, not for us lads,
With all these rioters: fanatics, zealots,
Religious maniacs.
They certainly keep us busy.
Overworked and underpaid, as usual.
But always interesting. Yes,
And every one is different. No,
I can't really complain.

I do not care
Whether my friends, like Simon,
Are shocked or amused, deride or bitterly
Accuse me of extravagance
In my display of love,
Or in my squandering of money.
I must do as I believe to be right.
I do not fear the living:
Their reaction is unimportant to me.

I have to live according to the law
My master taught me:
The law of love.

I do not fear the dead.
There is no money to be made from death.
My hands are accustomed to touch, to wash, to dry
The corpses of old and young.

4 A WOMAN

Many times each month
I lift the motionless feather
From another pillow where man or woman
No longer breathes.

Soon I begin the rituals of death
With oils and sponges, ointments and towels.
I work patiently
To the recitation of psalms,
Till the corpse is clean and simply clothed
In a plain linen shroud, perfectly clean,
The white garment that none of us
Will ever put on for himself
But all shall wear
On the appointed day.

Perhaps my accustomed closeness to the dead
Makes my bones ache
When the dark angel hovers near.
I felt him close to my lord
Whose body, I sensed, would be deprived
Of those rituals
Which are my gift to our people.
For my lord, I bought –
The price was beyond belief –
A little spikenard.
Nothing less than a king's perfume would suffice.
I mixed my precious aromatic
From the Himalayan valleys
In olive oil, as the law says,
(Only a priest of the temple need not do so)
And sealed it in a jar of alabaster.

While he sat at the table
Of Simon, our friend,
Whose leprosy he had healed,
I took my sealed globe of perfume

And held it above the head
Of my beloved lord.
He turned to me.
Heavy aroma of spikenard poured
Upon the air
As I snapped the thin alabaster neck.
Perfumed, strange, clinging
Drops of the scented oil fell
On his hair, on his face, on his clothes.
My king, whom I trembled to touch,
I anointed.
The costliest fragrance of the east
Bathed him.
He gazed down at me as I bowed, and
I knelt,
In the hushed, crowded room.
I sprinkled on his feet
The last drops of my perfume:
Gently I massaged his warm flesh.
Then I loosened my headband –
Decorum was irrelevant –
And wiped the remaining oil from his skin
With my long hair.

I was weeping
As I have never wept for any man,
Living or dead.
The perfume would cling to him for many days
Of life or of death.

I have to live according to the law
My master taught me:
The law of love.

I have given my life,
As a priest,
To the keeping of order.
There is nothing more important
Than the preservation of peace
In the holy land.

> You say a young man
> wants to see me?

Every year, during the weeks before Passover,
My clients report on all disruptive groups.
In the holy city
Peace is of supreme moment.

> He claims he can put
> one of those fanatics
> into our hands, does he?

Disorder now, in Jerusalem,
Would be blasphemous.

Distraught? They often are.

The crucial test is, of course,
In the narrow streets
When our people come crowding together
As they are now,
Thousands of families in the spring sunshine.

The healer who calls himself
'Son of Man'?

Family after family, family after family,
Herding in to make their home here briefly,
As our law demands,
Till they have eaten the Passover.

Frankly, he doesn't worry me
too much.

They cram themselves into every corner,
Happily huddled together
Like sheep in the fold.

Oh, messiah?

But easily aggravated, easily stirred –

For a mere thirty?
the old price of a slave!

Explosive under the Roman heel.

Yes, we should certainly
arrest him. See it is done.

8   A PRIEST

Every year I feel as Moses must have felt
Ordering the flight from Egypt!
Nothing must be allowed to hinder
The festival of creation and exodus,
Movement from chaos to order,
From womb to world,
Ritual offering of firstfruits,
Meat and grain,
In peace at Jerusalem.

I have kissed him.
Ever since I can remember
I have had my vision of the Messiah.
Now, it is being fulfilled at last.
I have snapped the twisted stick of humility
And pulled apart the thin cords of lowliness,
Not with my hands but with my lips.

I have delivered him up with my kiss
Under the gnarled olive trees,
For thirty shekels: the price of a slave,
Of the prophet who represents the Lord.

Enough of this dressing in rags,
Like Elijah disguised as a beggar
To test the worm-eaten hearts of men!
He who behaves like a slave,
Laying his hands on suppurating flesh,

Kneeling to wash feet
That have scuffed the ordure in ditches,
Will now behave like a king.

There has to be confrontation,
Violence of war, though only for hours,
A sudden blood-letting
Like the slaughter of the firstborn in Egypt.
I have timed it with precision
Fatal to the Romans
In our passionate city.
The night of the full moon
Darked by cloud
Will end in a blood-red sunrise.

At home in Kerioth, in South Judea,
When they hear the delirious trumpet-call
Announce the day of liberation
They will not yet know it was I,
A true son of Kerioth,
Who forced the Son of Man
With a kiss
To put off his ragged old grey cloak
And strap on his armour
Burnished for conquest.
But I shall become known,
I shall be honoured,
In Jerusalem and in Kerioth.

At any moment
I shall hear the drums and trumpets
And the screams of Romans dying.

When the Roman corpses,
Gashed and smeared with dirt,
Lie in the gutters,
And our Messiah enters the Temple in triumph,

He will pay tribute to my impatient bravado:
I, Judas of Kerioth, who saw the vision,
Chose the moment
And lit the dangerous flame.
I shall be chronicled
As the beloved disciple
Whose kiss heralds the new world.
It will be me that Jesus acknowledges:
Judas the Liberator!

And at the next Passover feast,
When Jesus has been king for a year,
Robed in purple and honoured,
He will give orders
For me to sit beside him
At his right hand.
We shall eat and sing.
Then, over the third cup of wine,
Before the blessing
He will turn and in the brilliant torch light,
While everyone gazes at us,
Pay me with a kiss.

Heartbroken
In the cold spring night
I warm myself at the brazier.
          Let the cock crow.
I do not know that man.
I do not want to know that man.
He has rejected me for my weakness,
Reviled me for sleeping in the garden
At the hour of his agony.
He demanded more
Than my body could perform.

Jesus wanted me firm as a rock,
Named me Peter,
But knows I am now even less than Simon
Who once obeyed his call.
I am sand.
I shall fall away,

PETER 13

Forget him, vanish
And long to be forgotten.

With James and John
Twice I shared revelation
And now experience death of the soul.

We exulted together
When the little girl,
A mere corpse on the bed,
Made the feather tremble with her breathing.
'Jesus is the lord,' we said, 'of death and life:
            Alleluya!'
She got up and walked.

James and John and I,
We marvelled together,
Heavy with sleep,
Awestruck, below the three shining figures
On the mountain.
Yes, we saw Jesus transfigured,
Our master,
Aloof in his radiance.
We worshipped him.
                'Alleluya!'

In Gethsemane,
James and John and I, under a clouded moon,
Whispered together.
Separated from the others yet again,
We shivered with expectation.
What third, final insight
Would come to us
Between the tents of pilgrims?
What revelation?

Only our sour knowledge that Jesus rejects us

Because we are ordinary men!

Why excite the spirit
If you know that human flesh
Cannot respond?
There is no alleluya.

How can you keep vigil
When your eyelids fall like a sodden curtain?
How can you pray
When your mind, overpowered,
Dissolves into sleep?

When your fingers by instinct
Clench your knife,
How can you hold back and not defend
Your master,
Not strike at the enemy?
Eyelids and fingers move
Of their own accord,
Like the tongue:
They are living flesh.
But Jesus rebuked me for drawing blood.
                    Let the cock crow.

To be a fisher of men
Was a crazy aberration.
Reviled for failures
I could not help,
I blot out the shining vision
Or, haunted by Jesus,
I might as well be dead
As go on living.

I am a catcher of fish
And now I return to my nets
Where I belong.

I do not care
If men gossip at the city-gate
And make my failure
The theme of drunken songs.
My faith is dead.
I have never known that man.
Let the cock crow again and again.

When I, the high priest, asked him:
'Are you the Christ,
Son of the King of the Universe?'
You heard what he answered,
Though his reply shattered belief
In the power of hearing:

'I am the Christ,
Son of the King of the Universe.
I, the Son of Man, am God.'

At this blasphemy
You do well to cry out,
Sharing my passionate horror.

As a sign of condemnation
I clutch my robe and, with abhorrence,
Rend it apart.

See, the fabric is destroyed.

He stands unmoved – it seems – by fear
At the thought of his death:
Of stones
Hurled at him to graze, cut, bruise, break him,
Stun and finally kill him.
How gently he smiles! Strange, strange.

One of my senior policemen spits:
Now two, now three policemen spit.
Their spittle meanders down Jesus' face:
His brow, his cheek, his beard.
Still he smiles. Bizarre!
Cover his face.

Hooded, let him be taunted.
Call on him to play the prophet now.
He says nothing.

Police of the temple,
Take him to the procurator
For a Roman trial.

If you wish to strike him
You need not restrain your blows.
There will be no reprisals
For a false prophet tormented,
No disorder in the universe,
No eclipse of the sun!

I have come from Caesarea to Jerusalem
To keep peace:
Roman peace in this turbulent city.
The zealots are increasingly violent.
But I shall prevail. I must:
I have no intention of being recalled to Rome.

Not for me a soft bed
In the palace of Herod,
I choose a soldier's rough billet
With my garrison
In the fortress of Antonia.
From up here, in this tower,
I can keep an eye on the temple court
Day and night.

My wife says the hawks are flying strangely:
A bad omen.
Feverish crowds of pilgrims

Throng and seethe like maggots
In a rotting carcass.
I knew there would be trouble this Passover
And there is.

These Jews wriggle, wriggle.
An ugly, infuriating race
To have to control.
I know them and I hate them.
But frankly, I would prefer this one Jew
To wriggle out.
I am unnerved by this Jesus.
Like any revolutionary
He looks wild, ragged, smouldering,
This so-called Christ.
But his eyes have a most shrewd gaze
That probes even the tough skin
Of an experienced Roman governor like me.

He explores my casual cruelty,
My weak callousness:
His gaze releases the poison within me,
He cleanses me with his eyes,
Cutting remorselessly all that is rotten.
I am unnerved and purified.

What does he murmur?
'You have said so.'
That is all I can get out of him:
'You have said so.'

And what does that mean,
In reply to my straight question:
'Are you the King of the Jews?'
'You have said so.'
Is he denying? accepting? rejecting?
Enigmatic. Then, silence.

But I know he is innocent.
It is obvious to a man of my experience.

Not another word?
To nail his limbs onto a cross?
Or, after a whipping,
To set him free?
I want him to roam the fields with his friends
And wander in and out of scruffy villages,
Curing lepers and blind beggars
With his hands that are never still
And spittle from his wide mouth.
I shall let him go.

But there have been complaints about me
At Rome. The Jewish elders whined:
'Pontius Pilate is clumsy, abrasive,
Unyielding. He *will* not understand
The way of life of the chosen people.'
And Tiberius told me:
'Play safe, if you want to keep
Your job in Jerusalem.'
I cannot afford to upset
Those whining rabbis again.

I had the gilded Roman shields
With Tiberius' name – and mine –
Hung up in Herod's Jewish palace
As a healthy reminder of Roman rule:
But the rabbis
Nearly got me recalled for provocation.
I had set up idols, they claimed,
For Caesar-worship. A shield an idol! But
Tiberius warned me: 'Be very careful.
Jerusalem is explosive.'
Explosive!
As if I don't know it, only too well.

We elders of Israel,
Expert in holy texts and shades of meaning,
We have been told to choose;
Not a word, not an interpretation,
But a life:
One man, named Jesus, to live;
The other man, also named Jesus, to die.

My lips choose, as they must,
With words from this real, dangerous world:
Jesus, the man of action.

I vote for the tough, shrewd nationalist,
Jesus Barabbas: athletic, glamorous
Leader against oppression,
With an agile body, mesmeric charm
And a knife red with Roman blood.
He is more popular

Even than that other Jesus,
The Jesus they blasphemously call Christ.

My lips choose Jesus Barabbas,
Son of an ordinary father;
Jesus Barabbas, man of the moment,
To help my nation writhing
In the grip of Rome.
The crowd will rise to him.

'Pontius Pilate,' I declare,
'Release Jesus Barabbas!'

But my mind, appalled, cries: 'No!
Let the dangerous man of peace go free!'
Jesus of Nazareth,
Jesus they dare to call
Son of the Father of All,
Jesus the brilliant expounder of holy writ,
Jesus whose moral demands
Point far beyond the holy law
And pierce the heart;
Jesus, most learned of teachers,
Wiser than Shammai, shrewder than Hillel;
Jesus, bringer of light
Into our dark tombs of the mind
To set us free;
Jesus, who makes me tremble at dawn;
My mind cries out to Pontius Pilate:
'Let Jesus of Nazareth go!'

But while my mind cries out,
The appalling rabble
Yell the chant I taught them:
        'Jesus Barabbas! Jesus Barabbas!
            Jesus . . . .'

A mob surges
Into the courtyard below: they yell, they roar.
But what is that rhythmical chant?

'Jesus! Jesus! We want Jesus!
Release him!'

Extraordinary! The omens were wrong.
That is precisely my wish
For this innocent man
With eyes that pierce me and heal me.
What? Listen again.
I can hear now – in the confusion–
The sickening yells for a Jesus – yes –
But another popular Jesus,
Jesus Barabbas. That fanatic!
A popular thug, a freedom-fighter,
A zealot with Roman blood on his hands.

The crowd chants:
'Jesus Barabbas! Jesus Barabbas!'
Oh no, he is not my Jesus; not my healer;
Not Jesus who is called Christ.

The Jewish priests, angry as wasps,
Hover and goad and menace.
A riot is seething here. The mob erupts
In the courtyard, with sticks and swords and knives.
I am not prepared to risk my job
Even for an innocent man.
Who would be?
The mob must be pacified.
Let them take their Jesus Barabbas.

And my other Jesus?
The crowd yells 'Crucify! Crucify!'
The Jewish elders threaten,
Demand Roman punishment.
Rome will expect me to act, and I shall.

But first bring cool water.
With an oriental gesture, unlike me,
I rinse my fingers here in sight of the mob.
Even those who can't understand my language
Shall see: I wash off blood with water.
The blame is not mine.
Now, I release that criminal
And I hand over Rome's innocent victim,
My enigmatic Jesus,
The only Jew I have ever liked,
To a whip that flays
And then
To the cross.
Take him away.

'You see this cloak?' I said to my wife,
'It's been worn by someone very grand:
A royal!'
'Go on,' she said, 'think I'm going to believe that!
You're teasing me again.
It's your cloak, silly, your new one.'

So I told her the guy who had worn it
Was a nut case
That the Jews call king.

Then we had a good giggle
And a few hugs
Till she noticed the dried blood-stains –
Quite difficult to see on scarlet cloth –
And that's when she began to get upset.

So I explained how it was all in fun:

But all official too;
How I really was on duty and how
The poor bastard's back and shoulders
Were bleeding anyway
From those metal balls tied to the whip-thongs.
His skin was hanging in strips,
His flesh was lacerated.
His back was a real mess.

'It's horrible,' she said, 'cruel:
And then you made it worse
With your mockery. You men!'

'Now look,' I said, 'we were only pretending
He was an emperor,
With a spiky crown like Tiberius
On the coins: only a few thorns,
Just a bit of a laugh;
We hung my cloak on him for a purple robe
And shoved a swagger-stick into his fist
For a sceptre.
We didn't hurt him.
Honest, I don't think it meant anything
To him. He looked very dim and weedy.
A pathetic specimen.'

Then she let fly:
'And who do you think you are, I'd like to know!
A real, bright, powerful Roman from Rome?
You're only a mean little local recruit,
A nobody from Samaria
Chucking your puny weight about!'

And that's when I saw red.
'Who pushed me into the army?
Who wanted me to try for Roman citizenship?
Who keeps on chivvying me

To get a recommendation
For a special edict in Rome
Signed by Tiberius?
You're the one,' I said, 'who's always been ambitious:
But over-sensitive and niggly as well' –
She's like a lot of Samaritan girls,
A funny mixture –
So I said to her, straight:
'You can't have it both ways.'

We made quite a rough night of it,
I can tell you.
Oh, it was all right in the end, naturally:
It always is. We had a good time
Before cock-crow. As usual.
And she really knows I've got to play along
With the system
If we want to get anywhere.

Of course she washed my cloak
To get rid of the poor bastard's blood;
And there's no trace of it now,
Not a stain. I bet
She'll have forgotten all about it
By tonight.

It was the wailing cry made me turn:
Up the road
A group of mourning women were lamenting,
But there was no corpse.
Only, between the Roman shields and red cloaks
A bent figure – stumbling under
A baulk of wood –
Staggered down the hill.

He fell three times before he reached me.
The women wailed louder at every collapse
And the soldiers
In their slow march
Grew more impatient.
'Here, come here, you black oaf!'
(Their commander was calling me)
'Come and carry this cross-beam
Or we'll never get to the north gate:

SIMON OF CYRENE I 29

Come on, pick it up!
Heave it up on your shoulder, man: move!'

I cringed away.
It was abhorrent to me.
I had never before
Touched any Roman instrument of torture,
Though of course I had seen –
As soon as we came to Jerusalem
For our first Passover
Since leaving Cyrene –
The upright posts
Standing ready day and night,
For the next wretches to be crucified.
I had shunned Golgotha after that.
I hate all violence. I always have.
We lamp-makers are peace-loving men;
And I was brought up
In a more civilised city,
Elegant, prosperous Cyrene.
There, the Romans hardly ever crucified
Anyone. But in Jerusalem
They compelled me to carry that cross-beam.

As I heaved it up
From their exhausted prisoner
Lying in the road,
The women wailed again and
The doomed man whispered to me: very quietly.
I could scarcely hear him
And his lips were as white as a shroud:
He asked me my name.
He thanked me.
He blessed me.

When I think that I have helped,
Even a very little,

To relieve the pain of my tormented
Saviour,
I give thanks.
That cross-beam was heavy, even for me,
And I am quite strong.

His blood, that had oozed
Through his clothes onto the rough wood
From his flayed shoulders,
Anointed my shoulders.
His sweat, that had poured onto the plank
From his head and neck,
Baptised me.

When I remember that I obeyed
His murderers
And did not protest
At the ritual
Of his killing,
I am anguished and distraught.

We old women of Jerusalem,
We have ourselves experienced the agonies
Of bereavement, of illness, anxiety,
Remorse;
Of love, accident, childbirth, sin and shame,
And then of yet more bereavement,
Death after death.

Our task is to relieve pain.
We come to the places where men
And women suffer, we come
To kill pain.
Oblivion in in our hands,
Even at Golgotha.

Through the heart of a man condemned to death
On a cross,
There flows black bitterness. The poison

Seeps and curdles and festers.
So, I say to the thief whose flesh
Will be pierced at any moment –
The soldier is standing over him –
'Drink this and blot out all your misery:
Remember no more
Before your life is wrenched away.
Forget all your misfortune.'
The thief accepts my cup.
He sips to find relief, to find
Oblivion.

I move to the first condemned man –
Three will be crucified today:
They must die before Passover –
And I offer him the cup.
In it, mingled with wine, is Arabian frankincense,
The sweet-smelling gum,
Merciful opiate to dull all senses,
To blunt all arrows of agony.
'Drink this.'

Then I hurry to the next victim
Of Roman justice as he lies
On the ground.
How can such a degraded
Man be labelled, even as a callous joke,
'King of the Jews'?
And I say: 'Drink this: it will give you peace.'
He will not. A little turn of his head:
No.
He rejects my cup. Such a refusal
I have never known before.
I am horrified, terrified.
How can he choose to experience
All that pain?

The soldiers push me aside.
'Woman, get out of the way!
You can't waste any more of our time.'

How can he choose the total pain
Of this vile death?
With a turn of his head
He has chosen complete agony.
How can any man choose to endure
This lingering, tortured end?

But I can do nothing
Except move to the third wretch
Before they nail his wrists too.
He drains my cup
With a curse.

I'm the lucky bloke who
Won this long black tunic
With a throw of the dice.
The cloth's filthy and bloodstained
Now, and even when it's been washed
No self-respecting king would be seen dead
In it: not even a phony
King of the Jews!
But it's good enough for us.

All these Jewish prisoners
Have to wear mourning when they're up
For trial, so this is what he still had on
When the time came to strip him
And get his crucifixion started.

Poor sod,
Just look at him!

THIRD SOLDIER 35

The flies are cruel today.
He must be longing
To brush them out of his eyes.
You can see his fingers twitching,
And his toes: but that's all he can move
And the flies crawl everywhere.

Well, I can't complain:
I've done better than any of my mates.
There's still plenty of life in this cloth.
His sandals are worn out, mere rubbish,
And his girdle is only a strip of twisted linen,
And his shirt is no better than rag:
But this cloth is good strong stuff.
No wonder my mates are jealous!

My wife likes black.
She'll enjoy wearing this
Till she's pregnant again –
We don't waste our time! –
Then I expect she'll cut it up and make it
Into clothes for the kids. She's clever
With her needle.
She may add a bit of embroidery
To brighten it up:
Flowers, birds, fishes. Donkeys she's good at.
Our little ones love that sort of thing.
All kids do, I suppose.

Yes, it's my lucky day,
No doubt about that.
I only wish we could hurry things
Along a bit for this poor sod.
I want to get home to the wife
And give her this tunic.
She'll be over the moon about it.

At first the soldiers would not let us come
Near to the cross.
'Get back!' they shouted, jabbed their spears,
Hustled us down the slope again.

'Keep away!' they jeered, 'Your king is too busy
To see you.
Obstinate bitches: go back!'

The soldiers let other people get near
To the crosses, to jeer and spit
And make vile gestures.
All we could do was wait.

His mother gazed and gazed at him
But we doubt whether she saw
Anything at all
Through her dazed, stricken eyes.

MARY OF MAGDALA I 37

I saw little myself of the taut,
Stretched-out limbs.

My eyes were seeing the past:
His gentle hands moving –
Practical, consoling –
And his eyes looking at me
With grave attention,
Years ago in Magdala . . . that day
When all my jerky, aching bones,
That I'd never been able to keep still
Or to move as I wanted,
Suddenly attained peace,
Moved together in
Harmony.
As a little girl I had been laughed at,
Left out, ignored.
Nobody would play with me.
I was never wanted.
As a young woman,
If you can't walk properly, but jerk about
And spill your food
And smear it on your face, of course
Nobody wants to look at you,
Nobody wants to talk to you.
Jesus looked at me,
Spoke to me,
Touched me,
Soothed me and healed me.
Years ago, at home.

How can anyone want to hurt his hands?
How can anyone want to kill his eyes?

No longer attracted by the pain
Of the men on the crosses,
The bored crowd

Wandered off home and the jeering
Faded. Then the soldiers didn't bother
Any more to stop us coming close
To the foot of the cross.

We have already waited an eternity
For him
To die.
How can she find the strength,
His mother?
Bewildered, she crouches here in my arms,
Waiting, waiting without any hope.

I do not think she has ever believed
In her son as the Christ,
Any more than her other children have believed
In him. Brothers, sisters, all of them shrug
Him off as odd, weird, mad.
But she loves him,
Loves him without understanding:
Her strange son.
That's what she calls him:
'My strange son. My strange son.'

But I?
I call him my Saviour.
Of course I don't understand him
Any more than she does.
But I know he is my Saviour.
I love him.
So we wait together, his mother and I.

I will not leave my brother.
I'll stick right by him
Till he dies on the cross.
The guards don't mind now:
They let me stay, as he's near his end.
Every so often, in this eerie darkness
And the horrible stench,
When the guards are huddled together,
I creep up to him.
I reach out my hand,
Flick the flies off
And softly touch his sweating body.
Even to feel I'm still here, to feel
That somebody does care,
Is a help to my brother.
So I touch him.

Mind you, I don't approve of him.

I never have. I know he's a thief,
A client of Jesus Barabbas.
They may claim to rob
Only the Roman bastards:
But my brother has always been
Unreliable.
Still, he's got a good heart.
He doesn't torture people:
He's not a bully or a murderer,
Like that one over there.
My brother is like our dad was: kindhearted.
He's done nothing worse than steal money.
But thank God our mum died years ago:
The disgrace of this would finish her.

Pain does terrible things to us.
Or perhaps it's a drug those old women give,
To help my brother on his way;
But just now I heard him whisper
To the wretch beside him:
'Hey! Will you remember me, sir,
When you come to your kingdom?'
Imagine that poor, filthy outcast
Owning a kingdom! A dung-heap, maybe.
But he replied, as if the words
Were being wrenched out of his rib cage:
'Yes, I promise. Today
You'll be with me in paradise.'
And my brother whispered back:
'Sir, I believe you!'
Crazy!
I heard him with my own ears.
Is it a game?
A mad fellowship in suffering?
Dying like this,
They can even pretend there's a future

For them!

I'm glad of this peculiar mercy
For my brother.
It does help, I suppose.

I walk in freedom
But grief imprisons me.
My clothes, my body, my spirit,
All mourn.
Self-accused, I wear my black clothing,
Ritual garments put on by each of
Those many prisoners
Whose trials I have calmly attended
As an impartial expert on the Law,
In the Hall of Hewn Stones.
Innocent or guilty,
All the accused must be dressed
In mourning there,
In the highest court of Israel.
And now I, so often the judge,
Find myself guilty, full of remorse,
Penitent and mourning.

I kept my new loyalty secret,
Concealed my belief in Jesus,
Hid it from my important, wealthy colleagues,
My fellow-councillors,
Devout Israelites like me
Who would have spurned me
For my new faith that searches the heart.

My powerful friends would have derided me,
My distinguished friends would have disowned me.
I am wealthy, respected:
But I am not a courageous man.
I dread rejection.
I hid my unorthodox allegiance.
Fearing what was to come,
I absented myself from the meeting
Where Jesus, I knew, would be accused;
I slipped home and left him.
My servants lit my lamps
And I studied the holy writings
While he was being condemned and tried:
Now, crucified.

Old Nicodemus, though he is bolder –
He dared to go to Jesus,
At least by night – Nicodemus
Sympathised with my timidity.
But I have come to Golgotha, to the cross.
I repent of my cowardice.
I am full of sorrow.
The real danger is over, now that Jesus
Is dead. But though I am still apprehensive
I have asked his mother – she is distraught –
To let Nicodemus and me
Take charge of his burial.
In her bewilderment, it is a relief.

I summoned my courage.
I hurried, a suppliant, to Pontius Pilate.
He granted me audience at once
And allowed me without demur –
Even without a paltry bribe –
To take from the Roman soldiers
At the cross
The body of my master.
It shall not be left to rot there
In the Roman fashion,
A corpse torn by vultures
And gnawed by wolves and rats.
It is safe
In the cave where I intend to lie
Myself when I am dead,
In my garden beside Golgotha,
Just beyond the city wall.

Evening would soon be upon us,
And Sabbath would begin.
We had to be quick,
Old Nicodemus, my three servants and I,
To avoid ritual defilement.
After the spear-thrust had certified
Jesus was dead,
The soldiers lowered the cross-beam.
We picked it up, and supporting
The rigid body
With a strip of cloth under his loins,
We hurried, jolting over the stony ground
Between the tombs to my own cave.
There, we laid it down,
Carefully withdrew the nails
From wood and flesh, wiped the skin with ointments,
Lifted the body from the cross-beam
Onto my white shroud

Which we folded to cover the face and limbs
And we hastened out, before
The first star could glimmer in the sky
Or the trumpets blare to announce
The beginning of Sabbath.

Now my servants, with a great heave,
Have rolled the stone across the mouth
Of my tomb.
Inside, the body of Jesus,
At last free from pain,
Lies at peace on the hewn rock, on
The stone of anointing –
Not even a bed of intertwined reeds –
Until the Sabbath ends
And the women can come, wash it properly
And prepare it for burial.

I eat unleavened bread and bitter herbs.
I dip my food in salt
And I think of our nation's
Release from bondage in Egypt.
I try to rejoice
But there is no joy in my heart,
No sense of escape from the prison
Of my cowardice.

When the soldier said:
'He's finished. So be off with you, women.
He's dead, I tell you. He's had it.
There's nothing you can do. Go home,'
We were so tired that all we could do
Was to stumble a few paces and crouch down
Among the rocks.

I cradled his mother in my arms.
Our grief was dry.
Dry.
There were no friends, no disciples,
Only us desolate women
Keeping watch again.
I tried not to think
Of the corpses of criminals
Piled up together
In one of the communal tombs,

Where I knew the Romans
Would fling all that was left
Of him.

An old woman passed by
And offered us a little bread.
We hadn't eaten for hours.
We accepted it gratefully.

Then a strange man, much agitated,
A wealthy Israelite, Joseph from Arimathea,
Came to ask if he could see about
A burial for Jesus.
Our anxious relief came in
An outburst of weeping.
When he had gone,
We huddled together again.
We dozed, and eventually slept.

We woke to see a group of five men
Swiftly carrying the body
Still nailed to the cross-beam.
This Joseph from Arimathea,
This highly respected councillor,
Must be a courageous man
To have braved the Romans.
We agreed that Joanna and I would come
At dawn, with all we would need
When the Sabbath ended,
To prepare the body for
Its true burial.
Then I went home with Jesus' mother.
She slept. For a long time we could not.
But I have no memory of that Sabbath.

It was still dark
When we got up and prepared

Ointment of aloes, yellow resin of myrrh,
Sponges and cloths and flasks of olive oil.
I packed the long-necked jars in my basket,
While Joanna heated the water.
When it was warm enough
We took our pitchers, and with Mary,
As dawn was breaking,
We walked through the north gate.
Golgotha was deserted: a grove
Of gaunt, bare posts in the misty dawn.
All three cross-beams had gone.

We made our way among the tombs,
Every one blocked with its massive stone,
Some squared, some rounded. We hoped we wouldn't
Have to wait long for Joseph's men
To arrive at the tomb of Jesus
And heave that stone aside
To let us in. We wanted
To get our work over and done with.
Then we came within sight of the tomb
We were looking for.
Oh no!
We stared at it with horror:
A gaping mouth of rock! Open! Wide open!

The huge stone had been rolled aside
In its groove.
Who could have dared to enter?
No Israelite would have taken the risk,
When even to touch the body
Meant ritual defilement.
The Romans? But why?
We ran to the tomb and peered in.

Somebody was there.
A young man in white clothing

Sat on our right in the entrance, on guard.
He shone. He inspired awe.
And fear.
We shrank away, terrified. He stood up
And spoke: 'Do not be alarmed,' he said –
Alarmed? we were petrified –
'You are looking for Jesus of Nazareth
Who died on the cross:
But he has risen.
He is not here.'
The man pointed to the stone of anointing
At our feet in the ante-chamber.
'Look,' he commanded, 'there is the place
Where they laid him.'
I stared at the bare rock.
Tears filled my eyes.
'You must go,' he said, 'And tell his disciples this:
"Jesus is going before you to Galilee;
There you will see him,
Just as he said you would."'

We turned and fled with our baskets and pitchers.
We ran back, all the way back to our homes,
Too frightened to tell a soul.

And who, anyway, would believe
A mere woman?
Only a man can bear witness
And hope to be believed.
But I, Mary from Magdala,
Too frightened until now
To describe that amazing morning,
Know that Jesus was no longer in the tomb,
The empty tomb.

Later, I took a little of that myrrh –
Those rich, shiny, yellow tears of gum –

Placed them in a small linen bag,
And hung it round my neck
On a silken thread.
In the hollow between my breasts
This hidden myrrh is still fragrant,
A living perfume.

I think, as night falls,
Of people lighting the lamps I have made,
And every flame I imagine
As lit from the life of Jesus
Resurrected.

It is many years since I carried the cross,
Then crouched at Golgotha praying
To be forgiven:
Praying, praying, weeping.

Ever since that day I have been Christian,
Even before the resurrection,
And my wife too.
Life is full of change:
We have been called Berbers, Greeks, Jews: and now
We are known as Christians.
Our sons, Alexander and Rufus,

Often tell my story at their meetings
And repeat my message of hope:
'I believe I am forgiven by my saviour,
And I have forgiven myself.'

Recently our old friends in the synagogue
Have turned against us. They have
Refused to speak to us again, ever.
We have made new, Christian friends,
Though sometimes we feel lonely,
As our Saviour did.

The clay of every lamp I make
I sign with a hidden cross,
Remembering how I was called
To help Jesus to his death:
And he,
Lying in the road,
Blessed me.